LIGHTHOUSES OF OREGON
A PICTORIAL GUIDE
Mini Coffee Table Book

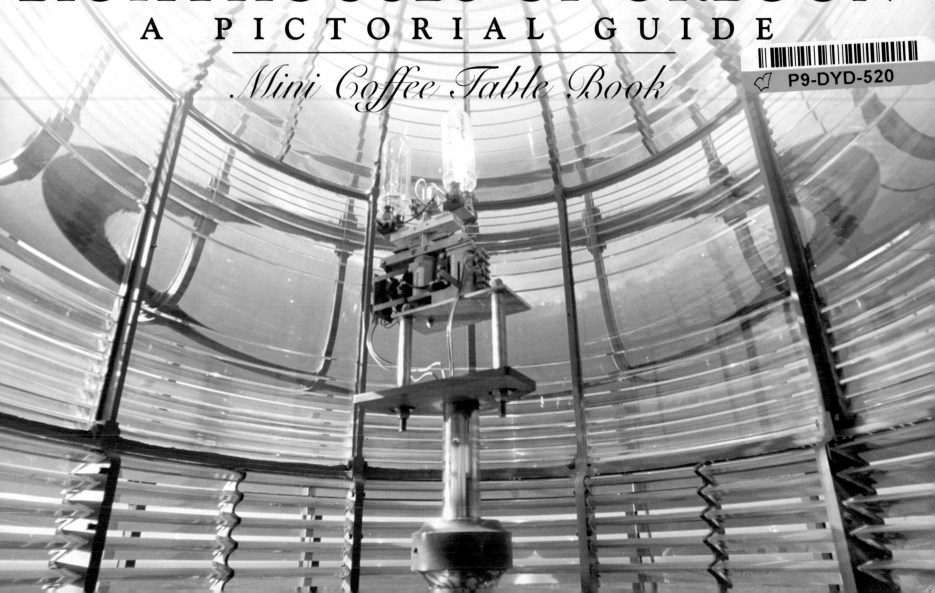

Welcome

Lighthouses have a special place in the heart of mankind. These often majestic structures have saved many human lives. The lighthouse is an icon of rugged reliability, probably more so than any other structure built by mankind. Lighthouses have been beacons, homes and refuges, and today remain symbolic of the world's maritime heritage.

Oregon's scenic coastline winds a path northward from the sandy southern beaches to the dramatic rocky headlands of northern Oregon. Along the way, the coastline is graced with nine lighthouses dating as far back as 1870, each with its own distinct characteristic in size, shape and architectural heritage.

When the Pacific Northwest became a U.S. Territory in 1848, Native Americans dominated the Oregon Coast. Along the lower Columbia and Willamette Rivers however, Oregon Trail immigrants were building settlements. With the discovery of gold in the Sierra foothills of California came the

opportunity for easterners to get rich quick. For most gold seekers, the only way to get to California was by ship. Eastern mariners were faced with many dangerous challenges at sea. The entire makeup of the Pacific coastline was very different from that of the East Coast.

Prompted by the need to protect the major industries of whaling, fishing and commercial trade, mariners have depended on lighthouses to safely guide them through treacherous coastal waters, inlets, harbors, bays and ports. Being an area of huge waves, high winds, towering cliff faces, rolling sand dunes and pounding surf building lighthouses here required extraordinary ingenuity and strength.

The geography of the Oregon Coast reveals massive sea stacks rising up unexpectedly from the waves out into areas of the ocean. Volcanoes in the region produced sharp, rocky points like knife blades. Swift running streams wash mud and gravel out of the mountains to form ship killing shallows and block off the entrances of rivers, where sea captains might otherwise find safe harbor from a storm. Although ships are built to withstand high winds and waves, most disasters at sea occur close to the shore, not the open sea. For as long as ships have sailed the seas, sailors have paid with their lives when their vessels came too close to the shore. Destruction and death wait where the land meets water. Unfortunately for many, such deadly encounters between ship and shore are common along the American West Coast.

With the increasing dependency on maritime trade, Congress launched an aggressive program to construct 16 lighthouses along the West Coast to help mariners navigate the waters safely. In 1853, construction of the first lighthouse began on the West Coast. By 1856, a powerful beam of light from Cape Disappointment stretched out across the waters offering mariners a new and safer way of navigation.

In the beginning, lighthouses were equipped with Fresnel lenses. These Fresnel lenses

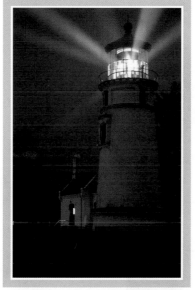

were made in a variety of sizes, otherwise known as "orders." The largest order, the first-order, measures six feet in diameter and as much as ten feet high. The smallest order, the sixth-order, is only one foot in diameter. The lenses were hand crafted and polished in Paris, France by one of the leading Fresnel lens makers of the time. Before electricity, an oil lamp was lit inside the lens to project a powerful beam of light. Because of the expense, high maintenance and care these lenses require, they have become almost obsolete.

Currently, automated beacons have replaced many of the classic Fresnel lenses. The Yaquina Head, Heceta Head, Umpqua River and Cape Blanco lighthouses are still in operation with the beautiful Fresnel lenses intact. In addition to helping mariners navigate their ships on course, lighthouses also warn them of impending calamity. In dense fog however, the most powerful beam of light can't be seen, therefore some stations added fog signals.

CAPE BLANCO ~ Port Orford 1870

Cape Blanco Light Station was built on 47.7 acres of land. It is the oldest standing and most western lighthouse on the Oregon Coast that has been in continuous operation. The lighthouse is the highest above sea, and the 59-foot tower stands majestically on a 200-foot cliff. Gusty winds and heavy rain are common to this area, and the rock terrain below is sharp and dangerous. Oregon's first woman keeper, Mable E. Bretherton signed on in 1903. Cape Blanco's history is full of shipwrecks. One notable shipwreck was the J. A. Chanslor (an oil tanker) in 1919. Of the 39 passengers, only three survived the collision with an offshore rock. James Langlois and James Hughes were Cape Blanco's most distinguished keepers. (Hughes was the second son of Patrick and Jane Hughes, whose 2,000-acre ranch bordered the Light Station property.) They both served their entire careers at Cape Blanco: Langlois 42 years and Hughes 38 years. Their job included keeping the light working from sunset to sunrise. The lighthouse is located approximately four miles north of Port Orford and six miles west off Highway 101 at the end of a scenic road.

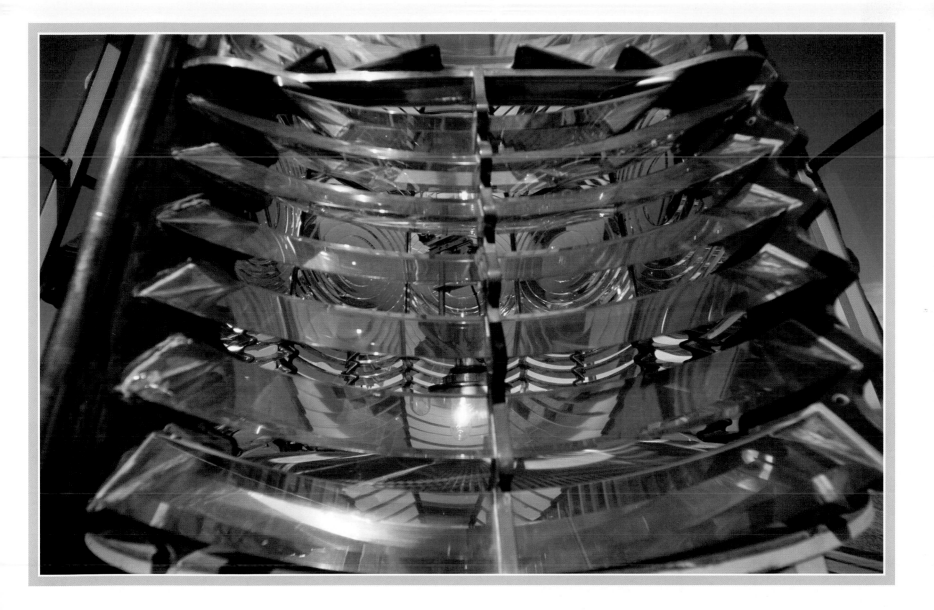

COQUILLE RIVER ~ Bandon 1896

In 1870, the schooner Commodore ran aground and broke up on the bar near the entrance of the river. Since the first wreck the list of the Coquille's victims has grown long and impressive. It includes many schooners, such as the Randolph (lost in 1915), the E.L. Smith (sunk in 1935), and the Golden West (foundered in 1936), as well as a large number of tugs and other vessels. Most of the unfortunate vessels came to the Coquille River to take on loads of lumber harvested from Oregon's tall virgin forests. The bar at the mouth of the river was considered by many to be among the most dangerous on the West Coast. In 1890, House Bill No. 6455 provided for the establishment of a lighthouse and fog signal near the mouth of the Coquille River. After a number of delays, construction of the lighthouse began in 1895 for a total cost of $17,600. The government engineers took advantage of Rackleff Rock, formerly peril to shipping. They blasted it level and set the new lighthouse on this firm foundation. The lamp in the fourth-order Fresnel lens was finally lit on February 29, 1896 with Lightkeeper James Barker in charge. He and his assistant, and their families, shared a duplex one-tenth of a mile north of the lighthouse The fixed white light, shinning for twenty-eight seconds with an eclipse of two seconds, could be seen for nearly 13 miles. The 40-foot lighthouse was active for only 43 years. Abandoned in 1939, an automated beacon replaced its duties. Open to the public, the lighthouse is a popular tourist attraction and is located at the end of a scenic road through Bullard's Beach State Park, two miles north of Bandon on Highway 101.

CAPE ARAGO ~ Charleston 1866, 1908 & 1934

Cape Arago's first lighthouse was built on the island's point in 1866. The twenty-five-foot-high lighthouse was an octagonal iron tower, supported by stilts. A staircase, exposed to wind and rain, circled inside the stilts up to a small watch room and into the lantern room. A low footbridge, built across the channel in 1876, proved too costly to maintain. It was washed away twice and in need of constant repair. In 1889, the Lighthouse Service decided to build a high bridge. The only surviving structures on the island today are the third lighthouse and the high bridge constructed in 1889 to provide access to the island. The current lighthouse was illuminated in 1934 and has a 44-foot octagonal tower rising only 100 feet above sea level. Cape Arago lighthouse is not open to the public and is guarded by a fence that is controlled by the Coast Guard. There is however, an awesome view of the lighthouse from a trail at Sunset Bay State Park.

UMPQUA RIVER ~ Winchester Bay 1857 & 1894

Umpqua River Lighthouse was originally situated along the Umpqua River. Constructed in 1857 in the Oregon Territory, it was the first lighthouse built within the borders of what we call the State of Oregon today. Listed in 1858 as a "brick tower rising from the keepers dwelling," it was 100-feet above sea level, with a third-order lens and a fixed white signal, first lit by Fayette Crosby. Major flooding in 1861 washed the first lighthouse away. The present lighthouse was completed in 1894 and fitted with a unique first-order Fresnel lens with twenty –four bull's-eyes, eight covered with panes of red glass which create a signal of two white flashes followed by a flash of red, timed equally by the rotation of the lens on a chariot base. Its 65-foot tower stands 165 feet above sea level and can be seen for 19 miles out to sea. The lighthouse is located off Highway 101 just south of Winchester Bay and is open for tours during the spring and summer.

HECETA HEAD ~ Florence 1894

In 1775 while sailing for the Royal Spanish Navy, Don Bruno Heceta set out from San Blas, Mexico with 45 men and provisions for a year-long mission to reach the Arctic Circle and claim points enroute for Spain. He made it as far as the Columbia River before turning back due to concern for his sailors who were stricken with scurvy. On his journey he noted the headland, which bears his name. Construction of the lighthouse began in 1892. Lumber came from local mills, the masonry and cement came from San Francisco, and rock used in the base of the tower was quarried from the Clackamas River near Oregon City. Laborers were paid $2 a day and worked an average of ten hours a day. The highest paid carpenter received $4 a day. One of the most awe-inspiring lighthouses to be found anywhere in the world, the 56-foot tower stands 205 feet above sea level and can be seen 21 miles out to sea. The lighthouse has been guiding ships with Oregon's most powerful light since 1894. It houses a first-order Fresnel lens with 640 individual prisms manufactured in England. For many years the lens rotated by a weight being lowered on a cable, similar to a grandfather clock. It was the responsibility of the keepers on the nightly watch to periodically rewind to continue the rotation. The biggest change at the station occurred in 1963 when the lighthouse was automated. A resident keeper was no longer required. Today, the station is the best-preserved lighthouse complex on the Oregon Coast. The trail to the lighthouse leads from Devil's Elbow State Park.

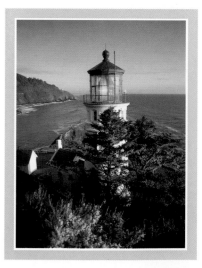

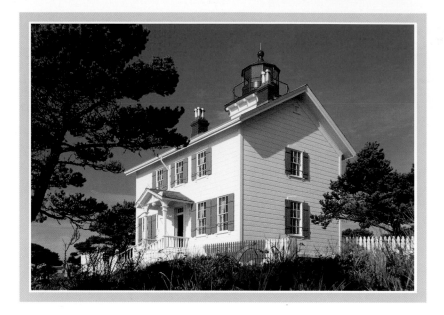

YAQUINA BAY ~ Newport 1871

Yaquina Bay Lighthouse, Oregon's oldest wooden-framed lighthouse and probably the oldest standing building in Newport, sits atop a bluff at the mouth of the Yaquina River. This sentinel, decommissioned in 1874, has stood the test of time. On December 7, 1996, it was officially restored as a privately maintained aid to navigation and recognized by the U.S Coast Guard with a re-lighting ceremony. Today the lighthouse remains in excellent condition almost one and a quarter centuries after it was commissioned. It's now a private aid to navigation. The original fifth-order lens is long gone and replaced with a 250mm lexan lens controlled by a photocell displaying a fixed white light from dusk to dawn and sometimes on dark days. The lens is a gift from author and former keeper, Mr. Jim Gibbs, until a fifth-order lens can be found. It remains an attractive historical Interpretive Center in Yaquina Bay State Park at the North end of Bay Bridge and is open to the public in early spring through summer.

YAQUINA HEAD ~ Newport 1873

Yaquina Head is one of the most beautiful lighthouses in Oregon. The tall white masonry conical tower was built in 1872 with some 370,000 bricks and is the tallest and second oldest existing lighthouse in Oregon. Its light is 162 feet above sea level, visible 21 miles. The lantern shelters an extraordinary nine-foot tall first order fixed Fresnel lens that is still used as an aid to navigation. The lens was made in Paris, France in 1868 by one of the leading Fresnel lens makers of the time, Barbier and Fenestre. It is now lit by a 1,000 watt flashing electric lamp. Originally the light came from a lamp fueled by lard oil. Keeper Fayette Crosby, who had been the first keeper at the Umpqua River Lighthouse, lit the lamp in the Yaquina Head lens for the first time on the evening of August 20, 1873. The lighthouse is at the end of a mile-long headland of ancient volcanic rock called basalt.

The lighthouse is part of the Yaquina Head Outstanding Natural Area managed by the Bureau of Land Management. Yaquina Head is three miles north of Newport off the Oregon Coast Highway, U.S. 101.

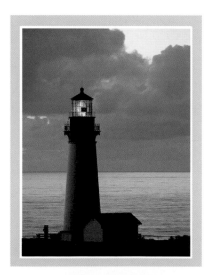

CAPE MEARES ~ Tillamook 1890

In March of 1887, Congress passed the bill to build a lighthouse on Cape Meares. Construction began in the spring of 1889. By September, the thirty-eight-foot-tall tower was completed. A first-order Fresnel lens, made in France, was shipped to the cape and was assembled in the tower by matching the numbers inscribed on the brass frames of each section. Its lens was comprised of hundreds of prisms, ground and polished. After the lighting apparatus was installed, a five–wick kerosene lamp provided the light source. The lighthouse, built on the outer edge of a high, bold headland, is 10 miles west of Highway 101 on the Three Capes Scenic Route in Cape Meares State Scenic Viewpoint. Cape Meares is the shortest lighthouse along the Oregon Coast. The focal plane was 223 feet above sea level and visible more than 21 miles. Cape Meares is named in honor of explorer John Meares, a retired British naval officer who set out to explore the American West Coast in 1788. The lighthouse was decommissioned in 1963 and is now a popular tourist attraction.

TILLAMOOK ROCK ~ Seaside 1881

Tillamook Rock is one of the most exposed stations and the only offshore lighthouse on the Oregon Coast. The lighthouse, located about 1.2 miles seaward off Tillamook Head, has received many batterings by violent storms. The 62-foot tower, 133 feet above sea level, was built on a basalt rock isle and is one of the most remote and least hospitable light stations in America. The lighthouse's flashing white light was lit for the first time on January 21,1881. The project of building the lighthouse on the basalt rock took three arduous years of fighting severe storms and rebuilding destroyed structures. There was a room for each keeper, a kitchen and a storeroom, which held supplies for several months. The expense of maintaining the battered structure over the years finally caused the U.S. Lighthouse Service to deactivate the lighthouse in 1957. Viewing is best from Ecola State Park, Cannon Beach, or Seaside, Oregon.

COLUMBIA RIVER LIGHTSHIP WLV 604

Lightships were floating lighthouses. They marked dangerous reefs and banks, or the entrances to rivers and bays. The first lightship to be placed on the U. S. West Coast was the Columbia River Lightship LV 50, stationed on April 9, 1892. In 1950, the present lightship was built by the Rice Brothers yard in East Boothbay, Maine and delivered to Seattle in March of 1951. From Seattle, the WAL 604 was sent to the Columbia River station, where she spent her entire career of 29 years about five miles off shore at the mouth of the Columbia River. In 1965, the Coast Guard changed the designated WAL 604 to WLV 604 and by December of 1979, the WLV 604 was decommissioned. She was the last lightship on the west coast to be retired. In 1980, the 112-foot-long lightship, powered by a 55-horsepowered diesel engine, was sold to the Columbia River Maritime Museum in Astoria, Oregon where she is still located and is open to museum visitors.